MW01047661

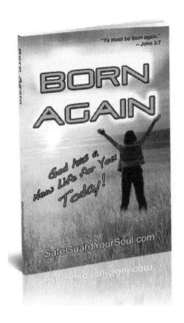

BORN
AGAIN

God has a New Life for You Today!

SafeGuardYourSoul.com

Born Again

ISBN-13: 978-1475122800

SafeGuardYourSoul.com
Frisco, Texas
Visit www.SafeGuardYourSoul.com

ISBN-13: 978-1475122800

Printed in the United States of America
All Scripture quotations deliberately taken from the Authorized Version of the Holy Bible, the King James Version

Cover Design by Bill Wegener at colorenlargement.com.

Do you desire to learn God's Word? – To begin receiving the *Moments with My Master* email that is sent out 2-3 times weekly, go to SafeGuardYourSoul.com and sign up. Or, email info@safeguardyoursoul.com.

Table of Contents

Chapter One

"Born Again?" Why?

Anyone searching for truth will find
an abundance of religion and religious practices in our world today;
all having unique and varying
views. Do the religions of mere
men meet God's requirements for
us to be adopted into His family
and go to heaven instead of hell
when we die? Is being good enough
by keeping the Ten Command-

ments what God requires? Just what does our Maker and Judge desire of us? When speaking to a religious leader, Jesus said:

"Jesus answered and said unto him, Verily, verily, I say unto thee, Except a man be born again, he cannot see the kingdom of God." John 3:3

"Marvel not that I said unto thee, Ye must be born again." John 3:7

Before we talk about the essential requirement, and definition, of being **"Born again,"** we must first have a clear understanding of our position in the eyes of a holy God.

Violating His Holiness

"All have sinned" against God,

says the Holy Scriptures and are thereby **"dead in trespasses and sins."** (Romans 3:23; Ephesians 2:1). Our sins have kept us from knowing God and being on His heavenly roll call. Why? God says that He is **"Holy, holy, holy"** and therefore cannot have a relationship with someone whom He has not yet made clean from their sin (Revelation 4:8).

"For all have sinned, and come short of the glory of God." Romans 3:23

But how is it that we have sinned against God?

"Thou shalt not bear false witness against thy neighbour." Exodus 20:16

4

Have you ever lied? If so, you are a liar in the eyes of your Maker and Judge whom you will soon stand before to be judged.

"Thou shalt not steal." Exodus 20:15

Have you ever stolen even one small thing? If so, then you are a thief in the eyes of a holy God and Judge of your eternal soul.

"Thou shalt not take the name of the LORD thy God in vain; for the LORD will not hold him guilt-less that taketh his name in vain." Exodus 20:7

Have you ever used God's name in vain? Have you ever blasphemed Your Creator with the words "God _____"?

"Thou shalt have no other gods before me." Exodus 20:3

Have you always put God first place in your life? If not, then you are seen as an idolater in the eyes of a holy God, the very Judge of your eternal soul.

"Honour thy father and thy mother: that thy days may be long upon the land which the LORD thy God giveth thee." Exodus 20:12

Have you always honored your parents? If not, then you are guilty of sin before God who gave you life through your father and mother.

"Thou shalt not kill." Exodus 20:13

Have you ever hated anyone? The

LORD says that if we have hate then we are murderers in His holy eyes (1 John 3:14-15). Have you ever despised someone in your heart? Have you ever been angry with someone without cause? Have you ever refused to forgive someone, showing them mercy even as you yourself are in desperate need of mercy? If you have committed any of these sins, then you are a murderer in the eyes of the Almighty. He alone is the very judge of your eternal soul. He will determine where your conscious soul spends eternity.

"That whosoever looketh on a woman to lust after her hath committed adultery with her already in his heart." Matthew 5:28

Have you ever looked upon a person of the opposite sex with lust? If so, Jesus says that you are already guilty before God of committing adultery.

"Thou shalt not commit adultery." Exodus 20:14

Have you coveted that which is someone else's?

"Thou shalt not covet thy neighbour's house, thou shalt not covet thy neighbour's wife, nor his manservant, nor his maidservant, nor his ox, nor his ass, nor any thing that is thy neighbour's." Exodus 20:17

If you have lusted or coveted after that which is not yours, God sees you as an ungrateful, sinful person. You will soon stand before Him to give account for your life and the sins you have committed against Him. He is **"Holy, holy, holy."** (Isaiah 6:3)

This bad news is essential. Keep reading and grasping these all-important truths friend. The light of salvation is just ahead.

At this point, you are probably slain, brought low, utterly guilty in your heart before God. You now begin to see just how sinful you really are next to His holiness and how in need you are of the LORD's mercy. That's a good thing and the essential beginning place to be. We are dead in our sins and that makes it necessary to be brought back to life again by the LORD.

"But your iniquities (sins) have separated between you and your God, and your sins have hid his face from you, that he will not hear." Isaiah 59:2

If you die in your sins – without having them forgiven – you will pay for your own sins for eternity in hell and the lake of fire.

"For the wages (payment) of sin is death; but the gift of God is eternal life through Jesus Christ our Lord." Romans 6:23

However, if you will repent or turn all the way to God in sorrow for your many violations against Him and accept the full payment the Son of God made on the cross for your sins, God will completely forgive all of your sins. At this point, you become reborn or born of God. The LORD gives you a new heart and this is the miracle He delights to do.

"For God hath concluded them all in unbelief, that he might have mercy upon all." Romans 11:32

We all must die and face our Creator and Judge. Denial of such a fact does nothing to change this reality. We are all facing death and then judgment and will stand alone before God on that Great and Terrible Day to give account to Him for our lives – all thoughts, intentions, motives, and actions. He sees all.

Born Again

Chapter Two

What We Really Deserve

"And as it is appointed unto men once to die, but after this the judgment." Hebrews 9:27

If you are reading this message and have not been brought to God through a born again experience in Jesus Christ, you are guilty before the Judge and in big trouble. The trouble you deserve, and that is coming upon you, is larger than you can possibly imagine and the effects of this judgment will never end. Let's explore what God fore-warns us to escape. But first, we should observe the reason we de-serve such a place.

Mankind is Corrupt

The depravity of un-redeemed men is a serious offense against a holy God. Before He judged the world in Noah's day, the LORD said the fol-lowing about mankind:

"And God saw that the wicked-ness of man was great in the earth, and that every imagina-tion of the thoughts of his heart was only evil continually. ... And it repented the LORD that he had made man on the earth, and it grieved him at his heart. The

earth also was corrupt before God, and the earth was filled with violence. And God looked upon the earth, and, behold, it was corrupt; for all flesh had corrupted his way upon the earth." Genesis 6:5, 11-12

Since God is holy, sin is a violation against His holiness and merits separation from Him which is spiritual death. Ultimately, that means separation from His holy Heaven.

"But your iniquities have separated between you and your God, and your sins have hid his face from you, that he will not hear." Isaiah 59:2

Jesus had many things to say about this horrible place called hell; where all un-redeemed sinners deserve to go. The Son of God revealed some details about hell that we should know. He even told us that hell was not originally created for us, but rather was **"prepared for the devil and his angels."** (Matthew 25:41)

Here's how the LORD defined this place called hell:

- Torment with fire and brimstone (Rev. 14:10).

- Weeping and gnashing of teeth (Matt. 8:12).

- A place of eternal remorse (devastating regret) .. Luke 16:25

- A place of torments (Luke 16:23).

- No rest day or night forever (eternal misery) (Rev. 14:11)

- A furnace of fire with wailing (Matt. 13:42).

- A place of everlasting burnings (Isaiah 33:14).

- A lake (ocean) of fire (Rev. 20:15).

- Unquenchable fire (ferocious flames) (Mark 9:45).

- Outer darkness (blinding loneliness) (Matt. 22:13).

- No 2nd chance to escape (utter hopelessness) (Luke 16:26).

- A place of sorrows (seething remorse and despair) (Ps. 18:5).

- A place of everlasting destruction (2 Thess. 1:9).

The Son of God actually voluntarily laid down His precious, sinless life when sinful men brutalized Him and nailed him to a cross to die. He did this because he loves us and does not want any of us to go to this horrible place of separation and eternal torment. Yet, all who die in sin, having not received God's forgiveness, will pay for their own sins in this place of torment. It's irrevocable. There's no second chance once one goes to this domain of the damned because the Bible tells us that **"it is appointed unto men once to die, but after this the judgment."** (Hebrews 9:27)

Born Again

Chapter Three

Judgment Day is on the Way

"And I saw a great white throne, and him that sat on it, from whose face the earth and the heaven fled away; and there was found no place for them. And I saw the dead, small and great, stand before God; and the books were opened: and another book was opened, which is the book of

life: and the dead were judged out of those things which were written in the books, according to their works. And the sea gave up the dead which were in it; and death and hell delivered up the dead which were in them: and they were judged every man according to their works. And death and hell were cast into the lake of fire. This is the second death. And whosoever was not found written in the book of life was cast into the lake of fire." Revelation 20:11-15

Horrible things are soon coming to this earth.

"The Lord Jesus shall be revealed from heaven with his mighty angels, 8 In flaming fire taking vengeance on them that know

not God, and that obey not the gospel of our Lord Jesus Christ: Who shall be PUNISHED with everlasting destruction from the presence of the Lord, and from the glory of his power." 2 Thessalonians 1:7-9

"For, behold, the LORD cometh out of his place to PUNISH the inhabitants of the earth for their iniquity: the earth also shall disclose her blood, and shall no more cover her slain." Isaiah 26:21

"And I saw heaven opened, and behold a white horse; and he that sat upon him was called Faithful and True, and in righteousness he doth judge and make war. His eyes were as a flame of fire, and on his head were many crowns;

and he had a name written, that no man knew, but he himself. And he was clothed with a vesture dipped in blood: and his name is called The Word of God. And the armies which were in heaven followed him upon white horses, clothed in fine linen, white and clean. And out of his mouth goeth a sharp sword, that with it he should smite the nations: and he shall rule them with a rod of iron: and he treadeth the winepress of the fierceness and wrath of Almighty God. And he hath on his vesture and on his thigh a name written, KING OF KINGS, AND LORD OF LORDS." Revelation 19:11-16

Let's read what Jesus told us is going to happen concerning the final days of this age leading up to His soon return.

"For these be the days of vengeance, that all things which are written may be fulfilled. But woe unto them that are with child, and to them that give suck, in those days! for there shall be <u>great distress</u> in the land, and <u>wrath</u> upon this people. And they shall fall by the edge of the sword, and shall be led away captive into all nations: and Jerusalem shall be trodden down of the Gentiles, until the times of the Gentiles be fulfilled. And there shall be signs in the sun, and in the moon, and in the stars; and upon the earth distress of nations, with perplexity; the sea and the waves roaring; Men's hearts failing them for fear, and for looking after those things which are coming on the earth:

for the powers of heaven shall be
shaken. And then shall they see
the Son of man coming in a
cloud with power and great glory.
And when these things begin to
come to pass, then look up, and
lift up your heads; for your re-
demption draweth nigh. And he
spake to them a parable; Behold
the fig tree, and all the trees;
When they now shoot forth, ye
see and know of your own selves
that summer is now nigh at
hand. So likewise ye, when ye
see these things come to pass,
know ye that the kingdom of God
is nigh at hand. Verily I say unto
you, This generation shall not
pass away, till all be fulfilled.
Heaven and earth shall pass
away: but my words shall not
pass away. And take heed to
yourselves, lest at any time your
hearts be overcharged with sur-
feiting, and drunkenness, and

cares of this life, and so that day come upon you unawares. For as a snare shall it come on all them that dwell on the face of the whole earth. Watch ye therefore, and pray always, that ye may be accounted worthy to escape all these things that shall come to pass, and to stand before the Son of man." Luke 21:22-36

Further, Jesus warns of these final days, telling us they will be unprecedented in all of human history:

"For then shall be great tribulation, such as was not since the beginning of the world to this time, no, nor ever shall be. And except those days should be shortened, there should no flesh be saved: but for the elect's sake those days shall be shortened." Matthew 24:21-22

This is God's earth, not man's, and He is holy and just. The LORD will therefore pour out His wrath upon mankind in an attempt to rescue as many as will call upon the LORD Jesus to be saved.

"Behold, the day of the LORD cometh, cruel both with wrath and fierce anger, to lay the land desolate: and he shall destroy the sinners thereof out of it." Isaiah 13:9

Eternal death and destruction are soon coming on all who have not made peace with the one true God who is going to bring all this to pass, just as He promised.

Yet, life everlasting with never ending joyous glory awaits those who know Him.

"But as it is written, Eye hath not seen, nor ear heard, neither have entered into the heart of man, the things which God hath prepared for them that love him." 1 Corinthians 2:9

The answer and the promise of God:

"For whosoever shall call upon the name of the Lord shall be saved." Romans 10:13

Now, let's talk about how we can escape the wrath to be poured out on the whole earth as well as eternal damnation in hell.

Chapter Four

Made New Creatures

"Sirs, what must I do to be saved? And they said, Believe on the Lord Jesus Christ, and thou shalt be saved, and thy house."
Acts 16:30-31

Turning to God in repentance and believing upon the only One who paid the full price for your sins is what God requires of us if we are to come into relationship with Him.

While dying on that cross for the sins of all mankind, Jesus uttered these three most powerful words ever spoken:

"It is finished." John 19:30

This means that the sacrifice for the sins of mankind was fully satisfied or "Paid in full!" The claims of the Father's justice to redeem mankind were satisfied completely by Christ when He gave His sinless life on the altar of the cross for the sins of all men! Of the Messiah, Isaiah wrote:

"But he (Jesus) was wounded for our transgressions, he was bruised for our iniquities: the chastisement of our peace was upon him; and with his stripes we are healed." Isaiah 53:5

Of this truth, Jason LeMaire testi-
fies:

"'It is finished" (Jn. 19:30)--When
Jesus said this He meant it--then
to the Father He went!! That's right,
when He shed His Blood on the
Cross, He bought me back-ON THE
CROSS."

Jesus Christ is the very Lamb of
God who took the blow of death upon Himself in order to ransom or
buy back a people for Himself and
His Father.

**"The next day John (the Baptist)
seeth Jesus coming unto him,
and saith, Behold the Lamb of
God, which taketh away the sin
of the world." John 1:29**

Will you be one of His people?

Made New Creatures

When we repent and place all our faith in Jesus Christ for salvation, all our sins (past and present) are remitted/forgiven and we are made new creatures for God's glory. His Holy Spirit comes to live in us. We are then His very children.

"Therefore <u>if any man *be* in Christ, *he is* a new creature: old things are passed away; behold, all things are become new. And all things </u> are of God, who hath reconciled us to himself by Jesus Christ, and hath given to us the ministry of reconciliation." 2 Corinthians 5:17-18

Those who are truly **"in Christ,"** which means they are truly **"born again,"** are **"new creatures."** The old sinful self is subdued by a miracle of God. He makes those who are His brand new from the inside out, cleansing all their sins, putting His Holy Spirit in them, and giving them a new reason and purpose to live. They are now made alive spiritually and become His temples the place where the LORD dwells (1 Corinthians 3:16). They have new life because Jesus is the life and **"he that hath the Son hath life!"** (1 John 5:12) This is the miracle Jesus calls being "**born again.**" *Nothing could be more important to any eternal soul.*

Chapter Five

Assurance of Salvation

"I know whom I have believed, and am persuaded that he is able to keep that which I have committed unto him against that day." 2 Timothy 1:12

Every truly born again believer knows he is saved. He has no doubt that Christ has made him a completely new creature. God has changed him from the inside out, washing away his sins and granting him a peace and love he never previously knew. If there is any doubt or confusion about whether or not you have been born again, this indicates that you have not been born again. Jesus said that it is a **"must."** We must be adopted by Him into His family (Romans 8:15) No one will be saved from sin and eternal hell by their own good works or religious activity or church membership or their standing with any organization of mere sinful men. Christ said **"Ye must be born again."** (John 3:7)

"He that hath the Son hath life; _and_ he that hath not the Son of God hath not life. These things

**have I written unto you that be-
lieve on the name of the Son of
God; <u>that ye may know that ye
have eternal life</u>, and that ye
may believe on the name of the
Son of God." 1 John 5:12-13**

The Bible tells us that **"God is
love."** (1 John 4:8) God's Word
tells us that we have **"all sinned"**
against our Maker and Judge and
are guilty in His holy eyes. We have
all lusted, stolen, lied, had other
gods before Him, coveted, hated
(murder), not honored our parents,
etc. Oh but that's not the end of
the story. Aren't you glad that Jesus had you and I on His mind
when He was shedding His holy,
sinless, and precious blood for us
on that cross? (Matthew 26:28;
John 19:30; Romans 3:23; 6:23;

5:6, 8, 9) Alleluia!

"Christ Jesus came into the world to save sinners." 1 Timothy 1:15

Keep in mind that not one sin will ever be forgiven by God UNTIL a person is in a relationship with Him due to being saved (born again). God will forgive not one sin confessed by someone who is not born again, that is, brought into His family His way—through Christ alone.

Do you want to know Him? Are you ready?

Do you want your sins completely forgiven? Are you ready for a new life?

Born Again

Chapter Six

Are You Born Again or Are You Religious?

"Ye must be born again." John 3:7

What does it really mean to truly have a relationship with the LORD and be **"born again"?** Why is this important? After all, Jesus declared that **"except a man be born again, he cannot see the kingdom of**

God ... ye must be born again." (John 3:3, 7)

You cannot and will not go to Heaven unless you go God's way and He plainly told us that His way is to be **"born again."** It's not about *religion* or trying to be good enough. It's about a personal *relationship* with the LORD, and this is what being **"born again"** is all about. Only the LORD Himself can do this miracle and He desires to do such for you.

John 3:16 says that God so loved the world that He gave His only begotten Son – NOT SOME RELIGION!

Most people who claim to be Christian are eager to say "I am a Baptist" or "I am Catholic" or

"Protestant." This proves that they are trusting their religion and not Christ who is the only Savior from sin and hell. They are lost. Being religious will not save you from sin and eternal damnation in hell – only Jesus Christ can do that. So, I want you to think for a moment about the very words of your own mouth when the topics of God, religion, or spiritual things come up. Jesus told us that **"Out of the abundance of the heart the mouth speaketh."** (Matthew 12:34) In other words, what comes out of your mouth reveals what is really in your heart. If your words have been anything resembling the "I keep the Ten Commandments," "I'm better than most people," "I'm a Baptist," "I am Catholic," "I was confirmed as a Lutheran," "I grew up Presbyterian," "I go to church," etc., it is because you do not know Jesus and are not **"born again"** as He said you **"must be."**

Concerning this dilemma, Pastor Mark Herridge Sr. writes:

"Most people today 'start going to church' but they are never 'Born Again.' They have never repented of their sin and they have not had a spiritual change. They 'add' religious duties to the old sinful man's schedule and mistakenly believe that will bring eternal life. Eternal life does not start when we get to Heaven – Eternal life starts when we were Born Again."

If your identity is in an organization of mere sinful men, you are doomed. Jesus Christ is not a religion nor did He come to the earth to start a religion. The Son of God is a divine Person of the triune Godhead and He came to shed His sinless blood to bring you into relationship with Him and the heavenly Father. This is what allows you the blessing of Heaven, otherwise hell is what lies ahead for you – and in hell all your feelings, faculties, and consciousness will still be there – forever (Mark 9:42-49; Luke 16:19-30).

*Now, let's find out what Jesus meant when He spoke of us having to be "**born again.**"*

Chapter Seven

Born Again: What Does that Mean?

Understanding the Born Again Experience

"There was a man of the Pharisees, named Nicodemus, a ruler of the Jews: The same came to Jesus by night, and said unto him, Rabbi, we know that thou art a teacher come from God: for no man can do these miracles that thou doest, except God be with him. Jesus answered and said unto him, Verily, verily, I say unto thee, Except a man be born again, he cannot see the kingdom of God. Nicodemus saith unto him, <u>How can a man be born when he is old? can he enter the second time into his mother's womb, and be born? Jesus answered, Verily, verily, I say unto thee, Except a man be born of water and *of* the Spirit, he cannot enter into the kingdom of God. That which is born of the flesh is flesh (1st birth); and that which is born of the Spirit is spirit. Marvel not that I said unto thee, Ye must be born again (2nd birth).</u>" John 3:1-7

The Bible speaks of two births, not just one. Every person reading this message has been **"born of the flesh"** – when your mother's water broke, you came forth and were birthed into the world and this is what is referred to here as **"born of water"** in verse 5 and also **"that which is born of flesh"** in verse 6. Being **"born of water"** or **"of flesh"** is the first birth, but to become a child of God and go to Heaven, one must be **"born again"** (again born) or experience the second birth which is spiritual, not physical. There is no other way. This is a non-negotiable eternal truth.

- **1st Birth** – **"born of water."**
Every human being is **"born of water"** when he comes forth from his

mother's womb (as her water breaks).

2ⁿᵈ Birth – "born...*of* the Spirit."
This happens as one is brought to repentance for his sins under the conviction of the Holy Ghost and chooses to fall upon the mercy of God through the shed blood of our LORD and Savior Jesus Christ who bled once for the sins of the world on the cross of Calvary. As that person confesses his sin and Christ as LORD, he is saved or born again. He arises a new creature in Christ and is never the same – he has a whole new life which bears fruit unto the LORD (2 Corinthians 5:17-18).

During His discourse with Nicode-mus, Jesus clearly refers to the natural birth when He talks about being **"born of water."** When a mother's water breaks, the child having been kept in that water, is then **"born of water"** or has been born once. Jesus then says that in order to enter His kingdom, that person **"must be born again."** Being **"born of the Spirit"** is a miracle only God Himself can do. Every human being has been **"born of water"** but must have a spiritual rebirth, being brought to life by Christ, raised from their spiritual dead state, to have a place in God's kingdom.

Every human being is **"born of water."** The mother's water sack holds the baby until the water breaks and the child is **"born of water"** or **"born of flesh"** or in the flesh which speaks of the first, the natural birth.

Concerning the past life of those who are now born again, the Bible says that **"you hath he quickened (saved, made alive), who were dead in trespasses and sins."** (Ephesians 2:1)

An honest reading of the whole **"born again"** passage (John 3:1-8) reveals that Jesus is speaking of the contrast between the *natural* and the *spiritual* birth to help us understand how one enters His blessed kingdom. Natural birth speaks of being born into the world as a fleshly human being. But THEN, after that human being is **"born of water"** or born into this world, they are born separated from God. This is why there **"must"** be a **"born AGAIN"** experi-

ence which is something only God
can perform and He desires to do
such for all. Many refer to being
"born again" as the second birth.
To be in God's kingdom, one
"must be" born the second time –
this time it's a spiritual rebirth.
Christ said that a spiritual birth
into His kingdom is a **"must."**
Without it, there will be no en-
trance into His kingdom.

Every human being alive today had
a *natural* birth but only some have
had a *spiritual* birthing into God's
kingdom.

Being born of the water is when the
mother's water breaks and that
person is **"born of flesh."** Being
"born of spirit" is the regenerating
work of the Holy Spirit when He
causes one to be born again (John

3:1-8; Titus 3:5-6). This is called **"the washing of regeneration, and renewing of the Holy Ghost."** (Titus 3:5-7) When **"born of the Spirit,"** we are made new creatures and our sins are washed away.

Realizing our own utter depravity and how we have violated God's holy Law, we must turn our whole life over to the LORD. When we do this He does a miracle in our hearts which is an internal work, not water on the outside of the body. H2O has nothing to do with that regeneration (being born of the Spirit) which is a miracle that only God can perform inside a man's heart.

Just "confessing Christ" is not enough. To be born again, one must fully and without reserve throw himself upon the mercy of God as a hopeless sinner. It's only then that the Father will regenerate that person, saving them from sin and certain damnation, granting them eternal life which begins immediately. Being born of the Spirit will always yield the fruit of a completely changed life – from the inside out. Being born again is the miracle of regeneration that only the LORD Himself can do.

The **"water"** Jesus speaks of here when He spoke with this religious leader has nothing to do with water baptism. When the mother's water breaks a child is **"born of water."** He is then **"born of the flesh"** and in need of the second birth or being **"born of the Spirit"** or **"born again."**

Recently I received an e-mail concerning being born again and water baptism. Here is a portion.

The person wrote to us saying:

> "How can you say that Catholics are not born again? I mean, I'm not a Catholic, but the Catholics I know are all baptized. You mentioned John chapter 3, and I read it, and verse 5 says that we must be born of water and the Spirit. So, according to Jesus, the way we are born again is through being baptized. The verses you mentioned from Titus also seem to point at baptism with the 'water of rebirth and renewal by the Holy Spirit.' If Catholics are baptized, then how

can you say they are not born again? Your statement doesn't make any sense to me. If we aren't born again through baptism, as the Bible seems to say pretty clearly, then how are we born again? What other 'water' are Jesus and Paul talking about in those texts? It sounds like baptism to me."

Here is the Response:

First off, no Catholic gets baptized (the Bible way), only sprinkled (doctrine of men) at 8 days old. The Greek word for the biblical experience of being water baptized is BAPTIZO, which means to *dip, submerge; to make whelmed, fully wet.* Baptism is a burial or full immersion. It signifies the complete im-

60

mersion of the subject into the
LORD and His death, burial, and
resurrection life. No child, below
the age of accountability, is found
being baptized or sprinkled in the
Bible. No person in Scripture is
found being water baptized before
believing fully upon Jesus Christ
alone for salvation and being born
again which is the miracle of God
inside of the person who repents,
falling upon His mercy while calling
upon the LORD to be saved (Acts
16:30-34; Rom. 10:9-13). Actually
sprinkling or "christening" is not
biblical at all but water baptism is.
But water baptism does not save
the soul. Water cannot and does
not save any person from sin and
eternal hell. Only the blood of Jesus can save a precious soul and
the only way to contact His blood is

through repenting and placing
one's faith in Christ alone (Acts
2:38; 3:19; 20:21; Romans 5:1-2,
9; Ephesians 2:8-9; Hebrews 9:22,
etc.). Water baptism is of no value
until one is first saved by the blood
of Jesus. This occurs by repentance and faith (Acts 20:21). All one
is doing is getting wet if he is water
baptized or sprinkled without having been brought to full repentance
and salvation which happens in the
heart of man and not by wetting
one's outer skin. Hell is full of people who got wet or "christened," in
the name of the LORD but did not
know Him which can only happen
by obeying Him and being born
again (John 3:3, 7). Anyone who
goes to Heaven instead of eternal
damnation in hell (there is no pur-
gatory) will do so by obeying the

One who is the only door to Heaven (John 10:1-9).

"Not every one that saith unto me, Lord, Lord, shall enter into the kingdom of heaven; but he that doeth the will of my Father which is in heaven." Matthew 7:21

The first and entry command of Jesus is **"Ye must be born again."** (John 3:7)

Realizing now that you are a sinner in the eyes of your Maker and Judge, is there any good reason why you wouldn't repent – totally turn to God – and receive Jesus Christ by faith? Is there any reason why you wouldn't receive **"the gift of God"** which **"is eternal life through Jesus Christ our LORD"**?

(Romans 6:23) If you are ready to lay it all down and receive Christ into your life as Savior and LORD, the next pages will provide for you just such an opportunity.

"But as many as received him, to them gave he power to become the sons of God, even to them that believe on his name: 13 Which were born, not of blood, nor of the will of the flesh, nor of the will of man, but of God." John 1:12-13

Chapter Eight

Your Time to be Born Again

In a moment of sincere solitude, get alone with God or pray with another true born again Christian. Take yourself away from all else to honor the One who made you, bowing your heart to speak in prayer with Him who is Your God and Judge. He is listening. In fact, He's the very One who orchestrated all of this and brought you to this place.

Just below is a model prayer. If you will pray to God sincerely and from the depths of your heart, with all that is in you, He will hear and answer and save you.

Your Prayer of Repentance to God to Be Saved

Heavenly Father, right now if never before, I come before You as a sinner, fully admitting that I have sinned against You in many ways and am guilty and worthy of Your wrath. I wish to settle out of court, before it's too late and thank You for making full provision for me to do just that. I here and now denounce all trust in my own goodness, good works, or religion of any kind. I am here and now repenting. I turn my whole being and life over to You right now. I am not worthy of Your mercy but You sent Your only begotten Son Jesus Christ to die—to shed His blood— for my sins on that cross. After He was buried for three days You raised my LORD from the dead whereby You made the only way for me to know You! Thank You holy Father! I now confess Jesus Christ as my LORD and Savior and believe You raised Him from the dead to justify me. I beg You to take over my life LORD Jesus. Please fill me with Your Holy Spirit. Lead me into the way everlasting! I love You Jesus and thank You for finding and saving me! From this moment forward, I will serve You. I will tell others about Your great love and how You want to save them too! In Jesus' name, amen!

What Now?

- Preferably with uplifted heart and hands, give forthright thanksgiving to the LORD daily for finding and saving you from sin and hell and for His glory and eternal purpose.

- Tell another Christian that you got saved (Luke 12:8-9).

- Find a group of Christ-centered believers who love God's Word and study it unceasingly.

- Be water baptized (Acts 2:38).

- Obtain a copy of the booklet titled **What to do Next** available on SafeGuardYourSoul.com.

- Read your King James Bible daily and talk with God in prayer.

Read at least two chapters every morning soon as you awake.

- Follow Christ to the end of your life (Matthew 24:13).

- Read articles, listen to audios and videos, etc., and sign up for the free email devotional at SafeGuardYourSoul.com so that you can learn and grow in grace as a born again disciple of Jesus.

- Get your supply of soul winning Gospel tracts and this book. See quantity discounts at safeguardyoursoul.com

SafeGuardYourSoul.com

List of Friends and Family to Pray for and to tell that You Got Saved and give a Gospel tract to:

_____

_____

_____

_____

_____

_____

_____

SafeGuardYourSoul.com

Let's grow in His grace and learn His Word together. Are you ready to go deeper? Sign up for free email devotional HERE. The ***Moments with My Master*** email is sent out 2 -3 times weekly for the edification of the body of Christ. Sign up at SafeGuardYourSoul.com or just send your request to: info@SafeGuardYourSoul.com.

For the latest resources, please visit

www.SafeGuardYourSoul.com

GOSPEL TRACTS Available

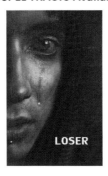

LOSER

Jesus told us all that only the losers will gain eternal life (Matt. 10:38-39). With the holy law to convict of sin, the necessity of "repentance toward God and faith toward our Lord Jesus Christ," and the holiness of our Maker emphasized, this Gospel tract has already blessed tens of thousands of souls with the knowledge of God. It's very well received among people. The ease of handing this one out is second to none. May God bless the conversations we are able to engage in when handing this one out to the lost and when supplying other Christians.

Read and Order Your Supply Today at SafeGuardYourSoul.com

Diary of a Dead Man

With the horrible cover image, this tract instantly grabs the attention of the recipient. While handing this one out, one may choose to ask, "That's a horrible image huh?" The person receiving the tract will then say, "Yes it sure is." To this the believer can respond with, "Please don't end up like that guy." This is also a very easy Gospel tract to distribute with wide receptivity – sure to make your seed sowing journey very fruitful.

Read and Order Your Supply Today at
SafeGuardYourSoul.com

JESUS: *Why Did This Man Die On A Cross?*

*With millions in print, the JESUS Tract is reaching thousands of lost souls globally and is perhaps the most condensed and complete presentation of the holy law and Gospel available in tract form today. This tract contains a glorious exaltation of the **"Great Shepherd of the sheep,"** the **"Good Shepherd"** who came to pay the complete price for the sins of His fallen creation (Heb. 13:20; Jn. 10:1-10). Order your supply today and begin using these messengers to reach those for whom He died and rose again.*

Read and Order Your Supply Today at SafeGuardYourSoul.com

SECRETS *From Beyond the Grave*

Shocking and thought-provoking secrets about the after-life. Contains a blistering menu of what awaits all who are not born again. This message is not for those who wish to hide the whole truth about eternal things. SE-CRETS is a tract few can resist reading with its aesthetic wickedness which reeks of death, and the curiosity pro-voking title. The message is 100% Gospel!

Read and Order Your Supply Today at
SafeGuardYourSoul.com

Order Your Supply of Soul Winning Gospel
Tracts Today at:

SafeGuardYourSoul.com

SafeGuardYourSoul

9201 Warren Parkway Suite 200

Frisco, TX 75035

469.334.7090

SHARPENING YOUR PERSONAL DISCERNMENT

For the Building Up of His Saints

To begin receiving the *Moments for My Master* email devotionals, sign up at <u>SafeGuardYourSoul.com</u>

Also, sign up for print newsletter on site.

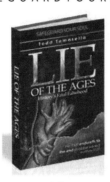

Born Again

Soul Damning Sins

Are there sins listed in God's Word that will damn one's soul to eternal hell? This is shocking revelation sure to strike the fear of God in the hearts of any who dare read this brief book. Great to read and to order copies to give away to others.

Find out more about this book at www.SafeGuardYourSoul.com

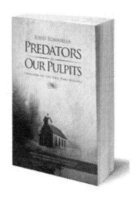

Predators in Our Pulpits
Invasion of the End Time Wolves

The prophesied great falling away is upon us – it's in our very "Christian" pulpits, books, and programs. As promised by our LORD and His apostles, "evil men and seducers" are waxing "worse and worse" in this late hour before our Savior's return (2 Tim. 3:13). Posing as ministers of righteousness, they have crept into the midst of biblically illiterate audiences on the wheels of their Trojan horse subterfuge and are promulgating poisonous pabulums in the pond of the heart of the people. These beguilers are depositing horrid heresies in the hearts of their hearers (1 Tim. 4:1-3).

Born Again

Millions are becoming casualties of their war on the God of truth as they feverishly prey upon unlearned and unstable souls. Our only protection from the father of lies and his emissaries is to go deeper into the LORD ourselves, learning His truth and walking in the Holy Spirit. The contents of this volume will greatly enlighten the reader and direct his steps down the narrow road of light and truth, ever deepening His roots in the King of the soon coming, conquering and eternal kingdom of God .

What should the God-fearing do in response to this epidemic of evil that has invaded the modern church? How can we discern *who* and *what* teachings are true or false? Discover these answers in this timely, epic volume permeated with rarely revealed truth sure to nourish and sharpen any heart that hungers for more of Christ and His righteousness.

Find out more about this book at
www.SafeGuardYourSoul.com

ANOTHER BOOK FROM
SAFEGUARDYOURSOUL

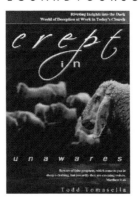

Crept in Unawares

"For there are certain men crept in unawares, who were before of old ordained to this condemnation, ungodly men, turning the grace of our God into lasciviousness, and denying the only Lord God, and our Lord Jesus Christ." Jude 1:4

The subtlety of the enemy and **"the deceitfulness of sin"** is never to be underestimated by the enduring and abiding saint of Christ (Hebrews 3:12-14).

> "And that because of false brethren unawares brought in, who came in privily to spy out our liberty which we have in Christ Jesus, that they might bring us into bondage." Galatians 2:4

The enemy of our souls is active and aggressive in hunting down souls as he preys feverishly upon them, knowing his time is very short.

> "Be sober, be vigilant; because your adversary the devil, as a roaring lion, walketh about, seeking whom he may devour." 1 Peter 5:8

Find out more about this book at
www.SafeGuardYourSoul.com

SafeGuardYourSoul.com

ANOTHER BOOK FROM
SAFEGUARDYOURSOUL

Raised Up

This volume centers upon the essential cross and resurrection power of the Most High, raising upward the bowed down disciple who waits upon Him in fervent expectancy of His divine life and soon return.

The call of God upon every believer to die downward that He might raise them upward to fruitfulness in His life and power.

"And the remnant that is escaped of the house of Judah shall again take root downward, and bear fruit upward." Isaiah 37:31

Upward fruit bearing occurs as the disciple takes root downward, being buried down deeply into the death and burial of Christ. The One who is **"the resurrection, and the life"** then simultaneously raises up that downward dying saint to newness of life in His Spirit (Jn. 11:25; Rom. 8:11).

Here is some of what you will learn in the pages of this volume:

- *How to sink down deep into the death and burial of Christ, that God might raise you upward to bear abundant fruit for His glory*

- *The importance of loving and honoring the LORD above self, and seeing His grace and power work in you in ministry to others*

- *How to discern which leaders are teaching the truth from the many wolves among us*

- *How to incorporate the cross in your personal life daily, and live a life fully pleasing to God*

The importance of prayer as you expectantly look for the soon and glorious return of the LORD Jesus Christ
In this poignant and timely volume, the person who is possessed by a self-serving "What's in it for ME" mentality instead of "How can I most please my LORD Jesus," is going to discover just how Luciferic his current views are. It is hoped that he will then be brought to repentance and a laying down of his life, that Christ alone might reign (Isa. 14:12-15; James 4:6-10). Ready or not - Jesus is coming (Lk. 21:34-36). Are you ready?

Find out more about this book at
www.SafeGuardYourSoul.com

ANOTHER BOOK FROM
SAFEGUARDYOURSOUL

Deceivers
and
False Prophets
Among Us

***THE BOOK SOME LEADERS HOPE YOU
NEVER FIND OUT ABOUT***

Are there false, fruitless and even deceptive predators in the pulpits of the modern church? If so, are these deceivers leading multitudes to the worship of false gods through their damnable heresies? Are "seeker-friendly" churches creating a new class of "Christians" who have no concept of authentic, Biblical Christianity? Are there leaders who are building their own kingdoms in lieu of God's and doing so on your dime? Are we hearing the full-counsel of the LORD from those in leadership, or the psychology and programs of mere men? Are beguiling emissaries in our midst drawing believers away from pure devotion and intimacy with Jesus Christ? Do these things exist within your local fellowship? Are you truly being instructed in the right ways of the LORD? Explore the answers to these and many more questions in this bold, insightful, and resourceful look at the church world today.

WHAT YOU WILL GAIN FROM READING THIS BOOK:

o   What specific erroneous teachings are circulating in the church world and how to identify and expose them

o   How to discern the genuine leaders who truly follow the Word and Spirit of God, from the false and fruitless who are using God's money to build their own kingdoms

o   How to please the LORD by positioning and establishing His written revelation as final authority in your personal life

o   How to discern and cease wasting your brief existence on this earth supporting wolves in sheep's clothing

o   How to serve God with a loving and concerned heart from the foundation of divine immutable truth

278 Pages

Find out more about this book at
www.SafeGuardYourSoul.com

Made in the USA
Charleston, SC
02 June 2012